Not all of me is dust

Not all of me is dust

Moira Lovell

UNIVERSITY OF KWAZULU-NATAL PRESS

Published in 2004 by University of KwaZulu-Natal Press
Private Bag X01
Scottsville 3209
South Africa
Email: books@ukzn.ac.za
Website: www.ukznpress.co.za

ISBN 1 86914 058 3

Editor: Kobus Moolman
Layout: RockBottom Design
Cover design: Flying Ant Designs
Frontispiece photograph: Sharon Bishop

Printed and bound by Intrepid Printers, Pietermaritzburg

The quotation that has been used as the title of this collection comes from the
translation of the poem, *Exegi Monumentum*, by Alexander Pushkin.
The title of the poem 'Tentless Rest' on p44 is taken from *Lara*, by Lord
Byron.

for Tony, as always,
and
Mamie, my Mother, on her eightieth birthday

Acknowledgements

My thanks are particularly due to Kobus Moolman in his capacity as editor for the University of KwaZulu-Natal Press; and to Elana Bregin, for her meticulous and empathetic reading.

Contents

Flight

I find myself awake in the dark vault
And all around are bodies horrible
In fallen face and sprawling limb and shroud;
My cousin Tybalt, further off, seems less
Transformed than some. Beside me, Romeo
Is still, though warm, and bears no signs of wounds.
I realise he's swallowed poison from
The empty vial that's settled at his feet.
(I recognise the brand, though miniature)
And kiss the vessel's mouth to drain one drop
That might deliver me to share his sleep.
But it is dry. A dagger lies before
Me on the floor. I weigh it in my palm:
It's plastic stuff, disposable, not fit
For cutting food nor piercing human flesh.
And just as I am wondering what to do
The voyeur sun, inquisitive, presses
A raddled face (as painted by Paul Klee)
Into my thoughts. Remembering the text
I feel I ought to make him go away –

A glooming peace this morning with it brings
The sun for sorrow will not show his head –

But all the bodies stir instinctively
To coming day and long before a switch
Is struck to fill with artificial light
The vault, they've shed their shrouds, and putting on
The masks of morning, wait impatiently
While air-hostesses pin their straying hair.

Meditations on Hotel Rooms

1

Life is the Bates Motel
You check in
Something takes you out
Perhaps just after
A confrontation
With self
Disguised as other
And the absolution
Of ablution

11

The sheet
Is a canvas
Splashed
With the art
Of creation;
The soap
An archive
Of pubic hair
In passing.

111

What does one do
But book a room
Indefinitely
Hoping that the
Advertisements
Have integrity –
That on a clear day
One can see forever;
That all one's needs
(And wants) will be met –
Though one suspects
That the sky will lour
And that curtains
Must inevitably
Be drawn.

Eliotland

Friday 6.15 p.m., London, July 1999

Outside the sun still browns
The warm breasts of the river
But I have descended
Via slabs of damp steps
To the unsunned Underworld
Where the unburied are ferried
In an odour of armpits
And a young man's unused lips
Are so close to mine
I can almost taste them
I who have just eaten cherries
On London Bridge
And thrown the pips
In the nippleless Thames
Eaten cherries on Eliotian turf
Jostled by thousands of lipless faces
On neck-stalks, body-stalks, stalks of legs,
Stalking talklessly

I had not thought Death had undone so many

Away from the clinking City
Into their Friday bloom.

Crypt

St Martin-in-the-Fields, London

The descent from
Too-alive London
Is cold brisk steps
(Past the chapel-niche
With the brown Christ
Hanging
And one candle
Lit by a passing prayer)
To the sepulchral crypt
Which is centuries-old graveplace
And new century grazespace.
Underfoot the tombstones
Are smooth illegibility
Save one
Which clearly bears
The pate and crossbones.
I select a roll
And glass of wine
(Body and blood over the counter)
Settle on a table
Crookbacked on chiselled stone
Confront a bone-white plate
And thighs of crossed cutlery
That leer at me
Proleptically.

Mkuzi Game Park

The Mamba, not among
Principal actors printed
In the programme,
Has a walk-on part.
He slides fatly green
Across the dust road
Sinuously insinuates
Himself into a tree
And conducts
From a slender branch
Singers resident there
In a shrieking
Dies Irae.
Of all the actors,
Principally
One recalls
The bit-player:
Silent soliloquist
Eloquent in motion
Bent with intent
Unlisted
Solipsist.

Rites de Passage

Harare, Zimbabwe, 2001

Beyond the townscape
Near the wicketing lawns
Where once you were lithe and long
In your cricketing clothes
And the waiters in white
Carried deference and trays
Clinking with drinks
Flat on their outstarched palms
                                    Now
There is only the morning smoke
Of early entrepreneurs
Rising in fire-shrouds
To hammer coffins – quality and cut-price –
Chisel the names of nobodies
Onto the stillness of stone
Plait into kitsch bright plastic flora
Drive klaxons of taxis
To the wailing wastelands
Where trenches queue
For the banquet of bones

Song of the Two Carved Lions

Zimbabwe, July 2002

For our lost roots

For the earth
In which once we treed

We who have been felled
And sculpted
Into
Some
Elselessness

(Knowing though
The knottedness
The gnarledness
Of sinewgrow
Of woody integritude
Before
This neo-leonine
New-entity nonentity)

Are nowdrowning
In a downgrowling
Of tears

Bloodwood

(the alternative name for the Mukwa tree, indigenous to Zimbabwe)

Lone travellers in a troubled land
Along this home-going road
We see boys in hubcap knees
Pushing wheelbarrows heavily empty
Past kilometres of clay pots crumbling
In tourist-dearth the death of barter-and-buy
See cathedrals of ribs
And in them curs long and lean-toothed
Tearing at once-fresh cow-flesh
While crows parson-kitted pick-and-pray
See woodlimbs in pile and pyre
On the bewildered earth
And two men rhythmic-axed
Bloodletting

(In the car are the two lions
Crafted in mane and Bloodwood grain)

And over the brooding granitescape
Scores of papery pods
Scuttle bloodless as ghosts.

The Tree-Felling

And when the time had come to axe the tree,
The old man said he'd do the job himself
(Like putting down an animal you've loved)
Because he was the one who'd planted it.
So heavily that day he took the blade,
Spoke gently to his friend a sombre while,
Caressing now and then its wrinkled bark,
Rebuking it for sending out its roots
To challenge the foundations of the house,
(Rebuking self for placing it so close);
Then gathering his age and strength and will,
He swung the blade and smote the sturdy trunk.
It shuddered once and shuddering dislodged
The axe which sliced into the old man's wrist.
The hand, it seemed, a moment waved farewell,
And then he fell, a log upon the earth.
Quite helplessly he watched his life spill out
And, drifting in delirium, he thought
He heard the roots, like echoing chalices
At Eucharist, receive the dark red wine.

Old Retainer

The fowls, assorted feather-dusters, flock
In reconnoitre right to madam's door.
Their owner, the old servant, biltong brown,
Has massed some mealies, set them on the march
In strong formation, straight as new recruits,
Across the stretch from kia down to house;
And house, it seems, has locked itself for siege.
Inside, the ageing widow sits before
A soft-boiled egg and sees reflected in
The silver of the songless dinner-bell
Past days: the servant padding, in starched white,
Along the passage on his pale-soled feet
To bring the clinking sundowners on brass;
And later, after dinner, padding out
In silence, with the clock alarmed for six,
Through gauntlets of dark orchards acres long,
To where his square room squatted like a stamp
Stuck firmly in its far right corner place.

House of Spirits

An effort has been made to tame the caves
With entrance fees and electricity,
And though they lie beyond suburbia
They're not beyond an easy Sunday drive.
The car-park is a bougainvillea blaze
Of orange in unruly tress and knot.
Reluctantly we leave the afternoon,
Descending into gloom on man-made steps
That exercise our city-sitting knees.
And suddenly the sapphire jewel appears:
A brooding pool the sun has access to
By Nature's whim – a skylight in the rock –
And shafting down, it turns the water blue.
It seems to lure, this sleeping azure here,
Though swimming is prohibited, declares
A sign in rust and several languages.
Persistently, a bird of strident voice
Is practising the rests and strangled notes
That constitute the solitary bar
Of song composed for it. Invisibly
But huge, somehow, and hovering, it screams.
Unstrung, we test the steely ladder to
A higher chamber forested with damp
And dripping stalactites, with stalagmites
That stagger up or stump, and somewhere, bats.
The wet floor is a premonition of
The flu to follow.
                              Still the dark bird squawks.
Quite suddenly the space is filled with flight
As black-limbed children wing in high-pitched squeal

Like bats detaching from their ceiling sleep
And flapping to the exit in a throng;
The ladder slows their movement, quickens fear.
A teacher, tweed and tired, waits behind,
A sheaf of science wasting in his hand.
'They tell me it's a house of spirits, this.'
And sceptical, he shrugs and slopes away.
The unseen bird is croaking somewhere yet.
We leave the dank shapes modelling themselves
In drip of sad eternity and glimpse
Again the aqua-gem inscrutable
In sleep.
        And when the air is bright enough
Among the tousled bougainvillea heads,
We open up the pamphlet that we bought:
It seems a hundred years ago a horde
Attacked the tribesmen here and flung the sum
Of dead into the sun-struck drowsing pool,
Which surely stirred a little and began
To shape them in its slow cerulean dreams.

Church

Dubrovnik, Croatia, July 1999

In the shrapnelled slab courtyard of the church
(Old Roman Catholic icon and baroque)
Behind a catechism of palings
One of the leanest of Dubrovnik's cats
Inside the carcass of a broken fish
Unpicks old flesh with flashing needle teeth
And steps from its own bone-domed cathedral
A bloat-bellied beast trailing oily prints
Where once worshippers were wont to pad theirs
(Before a war came and God disappeared).

Tabula Rasa

The staircase is baroque and we up here
Are gargoyles gawping at the atrium
Where Gidon Kremer stands among the strings
He has assembled from the Baltic States
To play tonight the work of Arvo Pärt:
The tablet scraped, a clean slate, it translates.
Shrills high as stridulant cicadas on
The oleander island where we swim
Precede the stillness of ellipsis …
Repeated shrill and still and tangled knots
Of strings like wire-wool scrub out the mind
Of what it was that held it so in thrall.
And scoured clean it shinnies up to where
A high-wire walker balances along
The taut compulsion of a single string.
At last we pass quite changed into the night
And looking up I see that even God
Has wiped his slate near clean, erasing all
Save an apostrophe, a sliver of
New moon, which cryptic punctuation clue
Would seem to indicate the Maestro's pique –
Possessive master of creation yet.

When firing was not acting in the night

Dubrovnik lurks below us in the dark:
We leave the empty airport and descend
On wriggling roads to where the hotel waits
For funding to rebuild its charcoal rooms,
Stark monuments to heated weeks of siege,
When Yugoslavs, Serb-driven, bombed the town,
Medieval big-walled bastion on the sea.
A private home will sheet us for our stay,
Its entrance hall an arsenal of shells
That spent themselves on other properties.
A little after midnight cannon fire,
Too proximate, untimely chars our dreams,
But waking we remember this is play,
And Fortinbras, atop the western fort
That rises from sheer rock formidable
In form, is soldierly in eulogy,
Proclaiming that the cannon clear its throat
To honour Hamlet, Prince of Denmark, dead.
The next night with our tickets we toil high
Above the whispering Adriatic wash,
Though far below the old star-startled sky,
To reach the fortress which is Elsinore
By night, by stagelight, by factitious mist,
Where conscript shipwrights labour through weekends
And bronze-cast cannons are being massed in haste
Against the hot Norwegian Fortinbras,
A youth whose soldier skills are still untried.
The plot unfolds replete with counterplots
Until at last the ordnance loudly speaks
For Hamlet's silence.
                              All Dubrovnik now
Turns in its bed reminded of the time
When firing was not acting in the night.

Memento Mori

One-time sirens of the city
Lie drying on the afternoon rocks
Salted by the assaulting sea

On the island cicadas sing
Plaintively as ghetto violins
In the ribcages of ruins

Though we are rested and ochrous
Dawdling by the translucent ocean
Our sandals are reliquaries

Holding our thin feet shrunken as
The rattling relics we've examined
In the treasuries of churches.

at fifty, in Prague

(after Vladimir Holan)

Stop your howling, Earth,
And muzzle those hungry teeth:
you will get your bones.

Dmitri's Dream

In order to reach the flaking walls
Of your blue apartment block
We must take the Moscow Underground
In Cyrillic incomprehension
Buy the evening meal from
Some pavement doeks who sell
Only the foliage of carrots
(More dental floss than food)
And trudge past aeons of melons
(Owners marooned among them)
To the thin door of the lift.
One by one we are hoisted up
The six slow floors
To your almost-empty room.
You arrange the fodder
On a plate of cracks
There is a jug of juice
You have bullied from berries
And in the corner
Posed as a photograph
Dmitri
In silent overcoat
And cigarette smoke.
We smalltalk
Through the meal
Excluding
Eavesdropping Dmitri
Until at last I say I'm sorry
He has no English

The outsider.
Oh he has, you say, *he wants*
To act Shakespeare
Famously in London;
He's here to hear you say
Pentameters.
From our mangled minds
We pluck portmanteau lines –
Put out the light, and then put out the light.
I come to bury Caesar, lug the guts
Into the neighbour room, a pound of flesh.
Of course
His ambition is absurd
(Though
No one Nureyev
Leaping through the bounds
Of nowhere
On will-power and potato
Landed firmly
Centre-stage
In the spotlight of the world.)
Dmitri's dream is *Hamlet*
I assume
Since that is everyone's
And he seems melancholy enough.
Nyet, categorically.
Richard Three, he says.
He spits out chunks of verse
Featly footing the iambics.

And then I see his crooked back.

Commentary

Days planned as poems
Devolve into the ploughwork
Of furrowing prose.

Yorick's Speech

Alas, poor Hamlet,
Holding in your hand
My stinking skull,
So unaware that soon –
Just beyond some swordplay –
The flesh on yours will set.
You know, of course, the process,
For you have dwelt much
On thoughts of dust
And metaphysics.
But still I am glad
That for me it is long over –
That first shock –
When the soul departing
Looks down and sees
Discarded there, the body,
Already skinned in the colours of decay
Rank
Oddly silent,
And slowly knows
That it, not that,
Is the eternal I.

The Suicide

World Trade Centre, New York, September 2001

Daily
He assessed
The fenestration
Of the building
Planning the fall
He might effect
And the finale
Full stopping on the pavement.

His mood descending
In the days of living
His spirit ascended
Floor-by-floorsomely
Dreaming of the height-thing, the flight-thing.

Then one September
While he was in waver-mode
Whether to die
Or what-the-hell-not-to
A hired bird-on-fire
Flew into his office-wing
(Worldnewsworthy, worldviewsworthy)
And he, fast-forwarded,
Farewell note unfinished
(Still composing his mind)
Fell into
Ellipsis …

Tattoo

Once, through lurching alleys,
Only the sea-heaved sailor
Sought (post-pub, pre-whore)
The semi-artist of the demi-monde,
Who, skilled in crudity and kitsch,
Would ink another port into his skin –
A souvenir to notch his docking
(Intermittently) in the unsalted world.

Now, in their non-conformist
(Copycatting) years, throngs
Of adolescents, already portraits pustular,
(All senses suppurating, pinched with rings)
Clamour to commit to inkscape,
Skinscape; vast canvases
For the cliché indelible
In intimate or extrovert display.

While I, till now unpatterned,
Posing in the studios of days
See, in easels of mirrors,
Evidence of the tattoo-maestro,
Nature, resolutely intent
On some premeditated design,
Some unsolicited masterpiece
Of chevron, wave and line.

Fireworks

When phony galaxies fluoresce the dark,
The holy stars, like hunted dogs ahowl,
Tuck in their tails to flee the firmament;
The moon, that solitary feline eye,
Disdainfully slides shut;
                                    Jehovah then,
The thunderous, asunder cracks the sky
With virtuoso thwackings of the rod,
And, sudden in his rage, engages rain
To douse the rabblerousers' fire work.

Party Poem

(for Tony, on his birthday)

I was going
To give you
A poem
But you wanted
A party
How alimentary I thought
How highly intestinal –
As I salivated
On the chewsomeness
Of a poem
The very peristaltic
Line-
By-
Line-
Of it
And the slow digestion
As it sits
Sometimes (I concede)
A little heavily
In the stomach
(Or the heart
Or the head)
Somehow Oliver Twisting one
Into wanting more

But
You wanted a party
So I have been
Onomatopoeic
In the kitchen
Drumming up the metalware
Working with lyrical anxiety
On the rhythm of the evening
Whether it should rhyme
Or fall in free verse anarchy –

How to whettingly
Turn transience into a
Memorable haiku –

Before the pentametric sonnet course
Which ought to (strictly speaking) be resolved
In rhyming couplet sweetly neat control
(Though omnibibulously tippling we
Might lose our footing rhyme and reason all
And trip the light anapaestic till we fall …)

It seems at last this party's at its close –
Let's start the poem before it turns to prose.

Evensong

In the evening
When you say it is time for
Walking the dog
I know you mean
It is time for talking to God
That is why
When you ask if I'm coming
I remain at my desk
Ordering the day into words
While you stalk the hills
Behind the house
In the silence of the dog;
And you know
That I am writing the 'I' out of world
And I know
That you are out walking with Dog.

Adam

All the while
Back-to-bark with the apple tree
I kept thinking –

Squatting convalescently
Nursing a troublesome ribcage
And an over-ripe tan
Naming from my limited lexicon
Miscellaneous fellow fauna
Sampling every root shoot and fruit
Other than –

That there must be more to life

Then I ate it (at Eve's insistence
She seduced
By the insinuating
Sinuous one
Lisping in
The hissing leaves)

Incurring
The Wrath …

Which in brief is:

Sweat
Forthwith
And
Forever

And
Death
(Unequivocally)
Eventually

So at last
I have
Something to do
In a day
(Imperatively
Because days
Are few and fleet)

And
I bequeath
To you
Death
And
Work

So that you too
Have daily
Something to do
And
A deadline

In the beginning

In the beginning
lurks the end
In the conception
the conclusion
In the carpenter
the cross
In Christmas
the crucifixion
In the crucifying
conceivably
the crux

Reason

If God gave
To Man
Reason
He gave to Man
Reason enough
To Reason out
The existence of
God
And having done that
Man is left
Searching
(Godlessly)
For Reason

Slivers

Naked
Under the knife
A potato
And in every sliver
A simple star
Like a gift from Heaven
To the growing Earth
So that those
Whose lot it is
To cut potatoes
May
Glimpse
In each
A galaxy
And God

Sleep

As the living
Lie down in bed

The dead it seems
Fly out of theirs

Flapping their way
Through sleeping skulls

Like powdery moths
In emptied caves

At cockerel-dawn
They're back beneath

A cold duvet
Of patchwork grass

The living though
Slough off their shrouds

As gavel time
Secures the sale

Of dark and star
To millionaire

High-bidding sun
But find their brains

This eye-rise hour
Are old projectors

Flickering dust
And decompos-

ing images

Wet

Watery, the world:
A wet Hadeda
Lifts his wings
As a swimmer would
His towel
And in a display
Of dazzling beakmanship
Preens himself dry.

But it returns –
The rain.

Statuesque, stoic,
Shouldering his wings
Like a military coat,
He stands
Head bowed
As at a funeral
The beak stilled
Dripping
Long
Tears.

Most Birds

Most birds
ablute
in the baths
provided
for avian use
but Hadedas
insist
on the swimming-pool
testing
the temperature
with
thermometer beaks
tentatively
entering
step
by ladida
step
breathless
with blah
as they
bosom
the blue
and shedding
their undergear
feather
by feather

Hadeda Madonna

(for Al and Mary, Christmas 2003)

No painted Madonna
More poised
No sculpted she
More still
Than this mother
Radiant in robe and rapture
Steeled in vigilance
Over a tangled wreath
Of twigs
Where the babe nestles
Feather-garbed and gaping
Wide
As our awe

Song of the Plastic Bag

(following its legislated extinction, May 2003)

Former body-builders
Muscle-packed
And stomaching
The food-bill
We have become
Deflating lungs
Floating
Consumptively indestructible
In the operatic wind
Towards a final aria
Composed on staves of fencing
In quavers of farewell.

Love-Song

Autumn woos me
Susurrating
With love-songs
Arouses me
As no other season –
The calm of it
The balm –
After the fisticuff
Full-frontal stuff
Of Summer.
The sky opens
Like a wide bed
The light is
Just enough
To read by
And the air
(Not yet a winding-sheet)
Woven of still winds
Is a fine cloth
To lie in.

Life

If the product is dust
Then the process is thus:
How to become the most
Efficacious compost.

Building

(for one who has died)

In droughtful times
The building opens
A hairline crack
Through which there is
Some sighting of a hearth
Though nothing definitive
As heart.
When the rain returns
Even mere drizzlespill
The crack clamps closed
And there is nothing to see
Save the fortitude of fortress.

Quite suddenly this Autumn
Something fundamental falters
And the fabric fragments
To dust.

From such motes
Mirages rise like monuments.

Horizon

(for my father)

Her father
Is floating
Supine and smiling
In the translucence
While she-on-the-shore
Is howl-mouthing
Seeing the horizon
Stretching like a finishing line
And he undulating towards it
Leaving her sanded.
Fear-fast-forwarded
She finds the future –
He supine on the furrowed sheet
Floating to the finishing line
And she beached
At his bedside.

Without you

(for Iona Stewart, on the death of Greig, in a climbing accident, 9 August 2003)

The three cats
Are looking for their stripes
In the ginger moonlight;

Dogs group
Like stalagmites
In a cave of nightness;

The horses in the paddock
Are still
As juggernauts
Stalled;

The distant mountains
Swing
Backpacks on their shoulders
And stride
Away.

'Tentless Rest'

(for Robin Hallett, who died 10 February 2003)

Soundless he has slipped
Through the flap leaving us to
Strike the empty tent.

Dormitory

Tread softly
Here
For the trees
Are asleep
Toes cork-screwed with cold
Dreaming
Of the last dance
The stripping off
Of umber gloves
In the stupor
That precedes
Stillness

'Not all of me is dust ...'

I found *Exegi Monumentum* first
In one translation, then a paler two
And felt frustration fuel me like a thirst
To read, *in Russian*, Pushkin, you.

How different is your confidence from Keats'
Who thought, as he lay dying young in Rome,
Consumptive-lunged and love so incomplete,
His name was writ in stream not stone.

You, not yet bleeding from the fatal lead
That spilled you slowly through your punctured guts,
Believed your wealth of wordplay would be read
Beyond your own disperse to dust.

And Keats was wrong because he's still alive
In Severn's sketch and his collected words;
And you were right, because you do survive –
Despite the bullet – in your hoard.

But what, I ask, will yet become of me,
So unproductive and past dying young?
The Keatsian image flows recurrently –
Of water and oblivion.